WHY

RITES OF RECONCILIATION

MATTER

To Jim Esler and Gerald Arbuckle,

who have a keen appreciation of reconciliation.

Why
Rites of Reconciliation
Matter

Gerard Moore

ST PAULS

Nihil Obstat: Rev. John Frauenfelder, STD
Imprimatur: + David L. Walker, DD, MTh
                        Bishop of Broken Bay
                        14 December 2007

The Nihil Obstat and Imprimatur are a declaration that a book or pamphlet is considered to be free from doctrinal or moral error. It is not necessarily implied that those who have granted them agree with the contents, opinions or statements expressed.

National Library of Australia
Cataloguing-in-Publication Data:

Author:	Moore, Gerard, 1956-
Title:	Why rites of reconciliation matter / author, Gerard Moore.
Publisher:	Strathfield, N.S.W. : St Pauls Publications, 2008.
ISBN:	9781921032875 (pbk.)
Notes:	Bibliography.
Subjects:	Reconciliation--Religious aspects--Catholic Church.
Dewey Number:	234.5

Published by
ST PAULS PUBLICATIONS — Society of St Paul
PO Box 906 Strathfield NSW 2135
http://www.stpauls.com.au

Cover design by Dorothy Woodward

Printed by Ligare Pty Ltd

ST PAULS PUBLICATIONS is an activity of the priests and brothers of the Society of St Paul who place at the centre of their lives the mission of evangelisation through the modern means of social communication.

Contents

Acknowledgments

I would like to thank the editors of *The Australian Catholic Record* for allowing me to rework material published in my article, 'The Forgiveness of Sins: A Ritual History', *The Australasian Catholic Record* 77 (2000): 10-19. Similarly I would like to thank St Pauls Publications for allowing me to adapt a chapter entitled 'Rituals for Forgiveness, the Rites of Penance and the Healing of the World' in *A Hunger for Reconciliation: In Society and the Church*, edited by Gerard Moore (Strathfield: St Pauls, 2004) 83-102.

Scripture quotations are from the New Revised Standard Version, © 1989, Division of Christian Education of the National Council of the Churches of Christ in the United States of America. The translations of documents of the Fourth Lateran Council and the Council of Trent are taken from Norman P. Tanner, ed., *The Decrees of the Ecumenical Councils, I & II* (Washington, DC: Georgetown University Press, 1990). The excerpts from the Vatican II Constitution on the Sacred Liturgy are from Austin Flannery, ed., *Vatican Council II: The Conciliar and Postconciliar Documents* (New York: Costello Publishing Company, 1987).

My thanks also to Richard Lennan and Dennis Nutt, who provided timely and insightful comments as the text was unfolding. My thanks finally to Chris Brennan at St Pauls for his work on the text.

Gerard Moore

Introduction

There is no reconciliation without forgiveness.

Nelson Mandela

Rites of reconciliation matter perhaps more than we realise. The Christian practices, rituals and habits of forgiveness and reconciliation help us deal with some of the most difficult personal questions and the most entrenched habits of the heart. They also affect the way communities large and small live together in harmony and peace.

We often have many difficulties with forgiveness. First, we find it hard to forgive others. Violence, betrayal, greed and indifference, whether towards us or another or complete strangers, can sear our soul, leave us calling for vengeance and retribution, and, ultimately, make us indifferent. The same can happen with smaller slights that often have a way of touching us deeply and colouring our thoughts, actions and relationships. Second, we find it hard to accept forgiveness. Sometimes it is just too challenging to accept the forgiveness and grace that is shown us. We can step back from love even when it is freely given, without strings attached. There is a third stumbling block: it can be very difficult to accept that another person has been reconciled and accepted back into the community, for example, when prisoners are released from gaol, having completed their sentences, but there are many similar instances in our own lives, including our families' lives. Jesus' parable of the prodigal son and the forgiving father wrestles with this difficulty in the attitude shown by the elder brother (Luke 15:11-32).

For two millennia Christians have pondered the scope of the forgiveness Jesus taught and lived. They have celebrated practices and rites that have enabled the faithful to forgive, to be forgiven, and to accept that God brings reconciliation even when we find it almost impossible to forgive. The history of reconciliation is the story of grace at work and a treasure trove of wisdom for Christians and, indeed, for all humankind. The basis of this book is to trace that history through to our present, offering a sense of how rites have mattered. Inevitably we will spend some effort studying the meaning of grace and the sense of sin. However our focus will be on the practices and rites across the centuries which enact the forgiveness and reconciliation that God has achieved in Christ and bequeathed to us in the continuous presence of the Holy Spirit.

We begin with a selection of passages from the Scriptures which open to us what Jesus taught and did – and how this was experienced, understood and recorded by the first disciples – as well as how, before the incarnation, God's forgiveness and reconciliation was a central component of familiar Old Testament texts. Our second chapter examines the Scriptures to see how the first Christian communities came to grips with forgiveness, sin and the reconciliation that Christ had brought them. These early generations in faith created rites and practices that continue to have a profound influence upon us. We share both their struggles and their solutions.

In chapter three we move away from biblical times to cover aspects across the first millennium. The period is characterised by the rise and decline of public penance, yet there is much more going on than this. An important development was the rise of 'penitential' spiritualities, best understood as practices and spiritual approaches that sought to bring conversion and reconciliation. This material is complemented in chapter four where we look at the emergence of private confession. Eventually the four basic elements of our contemporary practices of confession came into view: confession of sins, contrition, the completion of a penance, and absolution. Nevertheless this was a complex period, marked unfortunately by devotional practices aimed at seeking forgiveness for sins rather than celebrating the grace of Christ already so freely given.

The rites for the forgiveness of sin provide us with the focus for chapters five and six. Looking through the eyes of history, we see that the rite of confession has come to dominate our understanding of the ritual ways of forgiveness. Chapter five sets out the variety and depth of rites of reconciliation available to the church. This allows us to concentrate in chapter six on the four ritual forms for the forgiveness of sin found in the *Rite of Penance*. Furthermore we ask how these four rites should be celebrated. There are some interesting discoveries to be made.

The book closes with a discussion of the possibilities for dialogue with other Christian churches and for our rites to contribute to broader movements for reconciliation. It is important that Catholics recognise that they have something to offer society and that their struggles with forgiveness are a real contribution to reconciliation in our world. Yet, if this is true, then it is also true that we have much to learn from all human beings who attempt to bring reconciliation and forgiveness. In effect our rites call us into solidarity with movements for reconciliation and justice across the globe. We can see that rites of reconciliation matter within the faith community and across the human community.

Chapter 1

The Gift of Forgiveness
and Reconciliation

The first disciples were overwhelmed by a particular experience. They felt in the depths of their beings that their sins had been forgiven and indeed that the very power of sin had been overcome. It is important for us to recapture the freshness of this experience and the radical implications that quickly emerged. Yet as we take up this experience one thing needs to remain firmly in mind. The earliest believers, our forebears in faith, did not think for one minute that they had earned forgiveness or that they could master sin. Rather they were utterly surprised by grace. They knew that this was God's gracious work in and through the life, death and resurrection of Jesus, and that it was pure gift. God had reconciled them in Christ. All they could do was respond with a new way of living marked by thanksgiving and praise.

We will open our chapter with an exploration of how the followers of Jesus described their experience of the new forgiveness and freedom that came to them through his resurrection and sending of the Spirit. Our guide here will be the New Testament letters, especially those of Paul. This will be followed by asking how this experience was actually embodied in the life of Jesus himself, using stories from the Gospels, especially Luke. Finally, in light of these letters and Gospels we will re-examine some texts from the Old Testament to see how Jesus' own actions and words are in line with the ancient Jewish tradition. This will also allow us to rethink some of the ways we have used Old Testament readings to teach about sin without adverting to their lessons about God's forgiveness and love.

The experience of the first Christians

The first generations of Christians began to follow a wholly new way of living when, as adults, they were baptised and took up life in Christ. It is important to have a sense of the radical nature of their experience in its historical context. On the one hand, their excitement was infectious yet, on the other hand, remembering their historical context helps us to understand the origin and meaning of the concepts they utilised to think and talk about this new 'way', along with the practices and rites they established in response. So what was their experience?

For them there was the absolute conviction that they had been brought close to God through Jesus the Christ. Jesus was the way to God. With this was the certainty that God is loving, gracious and utterly committed to humanity and all creation. So close did they feel to the divine that they described themselves as the children of God. As adopted sons and daughters they understood Jesus to be their brother. Indeed they knew that God was continually with them, dwelling in history and creation through the Holy Spirit. Their hope was to live in the image of Christ, the Son of God, and in the power of the Holy Spirit, and so to be bound up in the love of the Trinity itself.

Salvation

From this set of perspectives how did they think about grace, sin and their newly found freedom? What did they mean when they used terms such as 'salvation', 'ransom' and 'reconciliation'? We will begin with the meaning of 'salvation'. In Christ, they felt they had been 'saved': 'There is salvation in no one else, for there is no other name under heaven given among mortals by which we must be saved' (Acts 4:12). The Graeco-Roman world understood salvation and the protection it implied as something that came from the emperor. *Now* this concept was attached firmly to God in Christ. For the first Christians 'salvation' implied forgiveness of any guilt, help in distress, protection from evil and demons, and the ongoing presence of the Spirit.

Living in a time when slavery was a commonplace, Christians also used this social practice as a metaphor to describe how sin affected them. They felt as if sin had captured them, controlled them and deprived them of their liberty. In baptism they experienced a profound freedom because Christ had snatched them away, liberated them and delivered them to a new household of love and grace: 'He has rescued us from the power of darkness and transferred us into the kingdom of his beloved Son, in whom we have redemption, the forgiveness of sins' (Col 1:13-14).

Ransom

Another important concept that the first disciples called upon to describe their experience was that of the payment of a ransom. It is much the same as redeeming a possession from a pawnshop, though the stakes are much higher. Because the payment of a ransom brought freedom the expression was used in Jesus' time to denote liberation. This freedom could be the very real experience of freedom from slavery, or freedom from prison or freedom from kidnappers. The idea of paying a ransom was also applied to the generosity of a donor who freed a family from a debt that was crippling them. When the early Christians reflected on their experience of being freed from sin they used this expression. Their newly found freedom felt to them as if someone had paid a ransom and their term of slavery to sin had ended. The sense of ransom was that they were no longer in the hands of criminals, with no control over their lives, but that they were generously restored to freedom and secure in the hands of their loved ones. It is clear that only God could be responsible for such a gift.

It is easy to see how this image was able to be applied to the death of Jesus. St Paul uses it as he reminds the Christians in Corinth to avoid being caught up once more in the slavery of sin: 'You were bought with a price; do not become slaves of human masters' (1 Cor 7:23). The payment of a ransom, then, is an important way of describing the experience of forgiveness and reconciliation with God. However it is crucial to recognise that this way of speaking is quite meaningless when pushed to explain the mechanics of how God has freed us. God is God and does not owe or pay a ransom to anyone! It is not a term that can be applied to God's actions but rather is an expression of how *we feel* when we realise that sin no longer controls us, that we have been forgiven and reconciled.

Reconciliation

A third notion that the early disciples called upon was that of reconciliation after a dispute. Here the presumption is that the dispute is serious and that the opponents are mutual enemies. The first believers felt that, before their conversion to Christ, they and creation were somehow at war with God, who, in turn, was hostile towards all the earth. Yet they now had the overwhelming sense that all hostilities were over, that friendship had replaced enmity and that a new time of harmony between God and humans had commenced. This was entirely God's work but one now entrusted to the Christian community: 'In Christ God was reconciling the world to himself, not counting their trespasses against them, and entrusting the message of reconciliation to us' (2 Cor 5:19).

The New Testament calls upon so many more images as it tries to express the meaning and experience of forgiveness and reconciliation. We have tried to open up three of these:

salvation, ransom and reconciliation. It is worth bringing a few of the points together. The key is that reconciliation and forgiveness are *God's* work, brought to us in Christ. We do not earn it, nor do we bring it about. It is an act of God's love, and it has been given freely to us. Following on from this, all the language we use to describe this gift should be geared to help us understand and appreciate more the experience of being forgiven by God. We require a multiplicity of terms, though we should always be attentive to how we use them. A good example is how the word 'ransom' is used to denote a sense of freedom related to a specific situation common at the time and so it should not be read as something that God somehow 'pays'. Another important point is that the understanding of forgiveness in the New Testament is attentive to the fact that sin disrupts the community and that harmony must be restored. In this sense God brings forgiveness and reconciliation.

Jesus forgives and reconciles

What was it in the life of Jesus that so touched his followers that they saw the face of God in the compassion and forgiveness he offered? In highlighting a few examples here we can see the breadth of the reconciliation he brought. The Gospels help us to see that Jesus had no illusions about human behaviour, taught the absolute graciousness of God, spent time in the company of sinners, reconciled known sinners, cured the sick, forgave those who harmed him, and was not afraid to name sin where he saw it.

In the first place Jesus showed he understood the way sin affected human society yet he did not turn his back on human failure. He did not seek out followers who would form an elite group that had no dealings with sinners. Rather he grieved with all humanity. This can be seen in his first beatitude, 'Blessed are the poor in spirit, for theirs is the kingdom of heaven' (Matt 5:3). A fruitful way of interpreting this verse is that 'spirit' implies our awareness and our thinking. To be poor in spirit is to have a mind and consciousness that is without any illusions about how the world is. With such a mind we see the suffering, poverty, misery, violence, corruption and pettiness that surround us. We also see that we have played a part in it. In effect, to be poor in spirit is to have the humility to know that we are finite and sinful, and to know that the world is in peril. Why does Jesus call this a blessing? The more we see the hidden workings of our world, our society and our own hearts the more we see as God sees. As God's love stretches to embrace all these and more, so we are blessed to love as God loves. It is a mixed blessing and not the easiest of graces yet this is how Jesus lived and loved.

Jesus taught the extent of God's love in the story of the father and his two sons, commonly known as parable of the prodigal son (Luke 15:11-32). We quickly see the misfortune that befalls the son who takes his inheritance, squanders it and then dares to think of only indentured service as a way out. Further, we are embarrassed and annoyed at the response of the older brother, who thinks that forgiveness renders his own dutiful and loving service unrewarded and wasted. Yet in many ways the story is misnamed. It is not really about the sons but about the father. He refuses to let go of what he loves, does not give up hope, accepts the repentance of his wayward child and shows the young man just how much he is welcomed back. Nor does he countenance pettiness. But just as he runs out to receive the prodigal, so he runs out to bring in the self-righteous older child. Perhaps this turn of events also reflects something of the scandal that Jesus' teaching caused to the self-righteous and the pious who were upset with his acceptance of sinners seemingly without punishment or cost.

Sinners found compassion, empathy, truth and forgiveness in Jesus. He forgave sinners and took pleasure in their company, something that moved and delighted the curious tax collector Zacchaeus (Luke 19:1-10). So comforting was Jesus' presence that a woman walked into the house of a prominent Pharisee while Jesus was at dinner there, washed his feet with her tears, dried them with her hair and anointed them with expensive oil (Luke 7:36-50). She sought forgiveness and found in Jesus reconciliation and peace. The forgiveness and healing that Jesus bestowed enabled men and women to return to a normal life after their deeds or misfortunes had previously led to their being ostracised by the community.

Jesus healed the sick and drove out demons. This is highly significant since, in his time, sickness and demonic possession were regarded as being directly related to sin. We see this in the question posed at the beginning of the narrative of the man who was born blind but who was cured by Jesus (John 9): 'Rabbi, who sinned, this man or his parents, that he was born blind?' (John 9:2). There is a telling counterpoint at the close of this story, as Jesus points out that the ones in sin are not the physically blind but the leaders who have eyes that work but no insight into what Jesus has brought (John 9:41). The supposed connection between sin and physical illness is also encountered in the story of the paralysed man who is both forgiven and cured when his friends lower him through the roof (Luke 5:17-26).

The many stories in the Gospels of healings were interpreted, then, as Jesus' willingness to bring peace to sinners and to restore them to the community. This was very important in a society where illness could render a person ritually impure, leaving them isolated from family and friends, driven out from society and, consequently, desperately poor. We meet this predicament in the lepers that Jesus healed (Luke 5:12-16), the woman with constant bleeding (Luke 8:43-48), and the naked, homeless man possessed by demons who once lived in the city but now finds shelter in burial grounds (Luke 8:26-39).

Jesus also forgave those who did him harm. He remained faithful to his disciples even while they misunderstood him and betrayed him, something best seen in the forgiveness of Peter, the head of the twelve (John 21:15-19). He did not shy away from his enemies amongst the scribes, priests, Pharisees, Sadducees and Romans. Rather he turned to Jerusalem (Matt 16:21) and wept over its hardheartedness (Matt 23:37). He forgave those who cruelly killed him: 'Father, forgive them; for they do not know what they are doing' (Luke 23:34).

Importantly Jesus named sin and challenged sinful behaviour. He recognises the sinfulness of the woman who washes his feet (Luke 7:47) though he does not name her sins. Something similar can be seen in his conversation with the woman by the well (John 4:1-42) during which Jesus speaks with her about her wayward behaviour. Yet in both these cases Jesus names out loud sinful activities that were already well known in the community. He is at his most fierce when he is required to name sinfulness that is cloaked in righteousness. He is found denouncing the hypocrisy of community leaders and attacking the scribes and Pharisees who use the Law to oppress people (Luke 11:37–12:3). He confounds the Pharisees who spend time watching and plotting – itself a sin – but who are stubbornly blind to the fact that curing a sick person on the Sabbath is in fact the fulfillment of the Law (Luke 13:10-17). Ultimately the religious authorities plan to have Jesus killed because he will not refrain from publicly challenging their duplicitous behaviour – a plan which, when it is accomplished, allows the people to see how their own leaders have led them falsely.

The Old Testament witness

Like Jesus, the initial generation of followers of Christ were Jewish and had a rich heritage – the Old Testament witness – to call upon as they pondered and rejoiced in the forgiveness that was now theirs. We share this heritage, yet we can too quickly overlook the ways that Old Testament texts bring forward God's love and reconciliation. It is worth examining three passages from this witness – admittedly a small sample but one, hopefully, which can shed light on many other readings from it.

We will take all three passages from the book of Genesis: the expulsion of Adam and Eve from the Garden, Cain's murder of his brother, and the story of the flood. On first examination they appear unlikely candidates for teaching about reconciliation. This is perhaps due to two sets of reasons. The first is that these passages are usually put forward as stories about sin. Ironically it is much easier to teach about sin than about grace. The second set of reasons relates to the use of these passages as stories of sin *isolated from their context*. As a consequence we are not attentive enough to the careful way they are incorporated in the single piece of work that is Genesis chapters 1 to 11. These passages certainly deal with sin but they do so within a greater context of grace, creation, forgiveness and ongoing divine help. This opening section of Genesis, chapters 1 to 11, was formed from a set of diverse stories, stories that were deliberately compiled, edited and adapted in response to the exile in Babylon (586-538 BC), one of the most disastrous periods of Israel's history. They were molded in the form we have them today not so much to condemn sinfulness but to provide hope amidst despair.

The expulsion from the Garden

The expulsion from the Garden is a strong image. In the story God is described as 'driving out' the hapless Adam and Eve, and placing fierce guardians at the Garden's entrance (Gen 3:22-24). It is clear that humans cannot remain in 'paradise'. Yet this does not mean that they are utterly contemptible or that God has thoroughly abandoned them. Before they are expelled they are clothed by God. Nor does God take back from them their newly acquired ability to know good from evil, a characteristic that we see as essential to human nature. Once established outside paradise, God continues to bless them, sending children (Gen 4:1-2). In turn the people respond, recognising that their fruitfulness is a gift, that they remain under God's blessing, and that the appropriate response is worship: 'At that time people began to invoke the name of the Lord' (Gen 4:26). It is clear that the story of the disobedience of Adam and Eve and their expulsion from the Garden is not simply about sin and some sort of divine wrath. Rather it is a complex introduction to the way God works to re-establish relationships which humans fracture. While the story recalls that our behaviour has consequences, it teaches that God's grace rebuilds us and that every human experience can bring insight when it is taken up in God's forgiveness.

The mark of Cain

Our second story, the murder of Abel by Cain, follows almost immediately upon the relocation of the first couple from the Garden to a new and fruitful place (Gen 4:1-16). Though barred from going back to Eden, Eve and Adam find themselves in a fertile country which supports children, fruit and fat lambs. At the same time the Lord remains close and on direct speaking terms. Again sin emerges and Cain murders Abel, in part out of jealousy but seemingly also as a response in a theological dispute. Our reading of the story often concentrates on God's uncovering of the crime. It is dramatic, with Cain avoiding any responsibility for his own brother and God uncovering the truth. The Lord's first response is to curse the farmer by both denying him his own living and using the very soil itself to remind him constantly of his wrongdoing: 'And now you are cursed from the ground, which has opened its mouth to receive your brother's blood from your hand' (Gen 4:11). Cain is sent into exile and can farm no longer. He is marked so all will know him. In the face of such punishment, how is this a story of reconciliation?

Already we can see that a process of reconciliation recognises that sin involves disruption and that some fairness and balance need to be restored. However the next several verses shed further light on God's approach. Cain cries out from his punishment and is heard by a God who had previously passed over his offerings. The sinner, a jealous, tempestuous murderer of his only brother, is neither silenced, nor ignored, nor despised. Though sent into exile Cain is protected by God, who 'marks' him as a sign to everyone that this man belongs to God and that sevenfold vengeance will be brought upon anyone who kills him: 'And the Lord put a mark on Cain, so that no one who came upon him would kill him' (Gen 4:15).

In a further twist, Cain remains productive. His wife gives birth to their child. No longer a family of farmers, Cain is described as the builder of a city (Gen 4:17). The curse on tilling the soil leads to a new direction, unleashing forces of creativity and vitality with unimaginable consequences for human civilisation. In all this Abel is not forgotten, and Eve gives birth to another child, also a son (Gen 4:25). When God is involved, reconciliation does not stop at punishment and rupture. In the story of Cain we see that the sinner is respected and placed under divine protection, that new possibilities emerge when all avenues seem closed, and that the victim and his family are not forgotten.

The destruction by flood

The narrative of the Flood provides us with a third insight into God's love and reconciliation (Gen chs 7-9). The sequence of events requires little retelling. The people fall into corruption and violence, God intervenes, the faithful Noah and his family are chosen as an island of refuge for the animals as God drowns humanity, and eventually life begins anew after the waters have subsided. Three points deserve close attention. The first is the ferocity of the punishment. This is not simply a flood. Rather it is an act of *un*creation. In the ancient world it was thought that the earth was surrounded on all sides by water, with the sky a gigantic barrier holding out the waters of chaos from above the earth. In the story God 'opens' the windows in the sky letting chaos in from above and, as well, 'unplugs' the fountains so that water bursts up through the flat earth from below.

The second point to note is the nature of the agreement that God makes with Noah and the earth itself. The God who is all powerful pledges complete fidelity to humanity and creation. There shall be no other flood, no other act of abandonment of creation. Rather, God sets down his warrior's bow as a sign of peace. Consequently, as rain clouds make the bow appear they provide a reminder to God that the earth is not be destroyed by flood again (Gen 9:8-17). In the light of divine reconciliation the rainbow is set as a symbol that God will not abandon humanity or creation, and will remain faithful to it no matter what. It is set as a sign that God's love remains constant, dogged, unfailing, and that grace prevails.

The third point is the unsurprising one that the humans do not seem to have learnt from the experience, with Noah's own family soon enough transgressing the boundaries of right and wrong (Gen 9:20-27). Ultimately the story of the flood is not so much about the flood waters or the ark but about the rainbow.

Conclusion

We will close our discussion of the biblical grounds for reconciliation with one of the most moving stories of the forgiveness that Jesus offered. It is also one of the most controversial. The event is that of the woman caught in adultery, found in the Gospel of John (John 7:53–8:11). The story is familiar. A woman has been caught and publicly exposed for committing adultery. Dragged before the people crowded around Jesus as he teaches one morning, she is used by the scribes and Pharisees as they pursue Jesus. Her plight offers them a chance to challenge whether Jesus will be faithful to the Law of Moses by concurring with their lawful desire to have the crowd set upon her with stones. The trap is set tight, given that Jesus is teaching in the Temple, surely a holy centre of obedience to the heritage of Moses, and that the people have already come to hear Jesus teach the law. In response Jesus turns the tables. His challenge that the person who has not sinned throw the first stone brands them as sinners too. Finally when the crowd has evaporated he treats the woman as a fellow human being, shows compassion and understanding, allows her to speak, and, in forgiving her, he calls her to a new way of living. It is clear that a new light has dawned at the Temple this day.

Why was this story so controversial for the first Christians? It is important not to limit the story to its being about only the forgiveness of an adulteress. There is sin in the way the leaders use the Law of God, the Temple, the gathered crowd and the unfortunate woman as a platform from which to humiliate and destroy a godly teacher and prophet. This is an abuse of their power and learning – something of a sacrilege. There is a sadness in the way the bullies melt away rather than choose to sit and learn. Their hardheartedness is chilling. Yet the early believers would have been familiar with the corruption that existed within the religious leadership. Rather than all this, what seemed most astounding to the early disciples was that Jesus could forgive so openly the terrible crime of adultery. We can catch a glimpse of their astonishment by looking at the earliest manuscripts of the Gospels. Scholars point out that the story was added at this spot in John after the text of the Gospel had been more or less completed. Other early manuscripts show the story at different places in John and even in an earlier edition of the Gospel of Luke. This shows two things. The first is that the story caused unease in the Christian community because Jesus was seen as too forgiving. The second is that, because the event described such a powerful act of Jesus, the community felt compelled to preserve it. In a sense it nagged at their consciences and collective memory. After some centuries the passage was placed where we now have it, leaving us still open jawed at the boldness and courage of Jesus' compassion. For our purposes the story sets the scene for the way reconciliation was understood following the death of the first generations of believers and as the Christian communities in the first centuries undertook the task of forgiveness.

New generations in different cultures and historical contexts have had to grapple with applying the gift that Jesus has left them: 'Receive the Holy Spirit. If you forgive the sins of any, they are forgiven them; if you retain the sins of any, they are retained' (John 20:22-23).

Chapter 2

Reconciliation in the
Time of the Apostles

Jesus left his followers the overwhelming gift of forgiveness. Yet with it came a simple problem, one that we still have today. How did the early communities take up the forgiveness and reconciliation that they had been given? Sin has been defeated and nothing is beyond the loving embrace of God. But how did the faithful enter this embrace? We will begin this chapter by examining the practices introduced by Christians living in the period of the New Testament.

It is worth keeping three points firmly in mind. The first is that sin, forgiveness and reconciliation are seen and felt differently by different peoples and cultures across the different ages. Consequently, when the faithful feel that a church practice of reconciliation is no longer effective, they abandon it. Some practices are retrieved later in history while others fall into long-term neglect. On the other hand, when the faithful find a cultural practice that they think could be expressive of God's mercy they introduce it to the church. Behind these movements is the principle that any rite must bring the sinner, in his or her own time, culture and language, into touch with the experience of God's loving forgiveness. When a rite no longer does this then it is not making present the reconciliation that Jesus brought.

The second point is a more theological one. We can be tempted to see rites of reconciliation as ways of 'winning' God's forgiveness. Nothing could be further from the truth.

We have been forgiven by God, so it is pointless to try to earn it. Nor could it have been bought or earned, since it is a full gift of God, given generously and freely. Rites and forms for reconciliation are to enable us to take up the gift of forgiveness.

The third point is that the sin of each person affects the whole community. We see this point come out when Paul writes to the Corinthians, explaining how all Christians are interconnected like the parts of a human body (1 Cor 12). In particular, he notes: 'If one member suffers, all suffer together with it; if one member is honored, all rejoice together with it' (1 Cor 12:26). Applying this passage to our sinfulness as well, we can say: when one member sins all feel the effect of the sin, and when one member is forgiven all are called to enter the new relationship in reconciliation. Sin, then, is not only an individual affair, nor is reconciliation.

The great reconciliation: baptism

The first ritual form that encompassed the forgiveness of sins was baptism. We find a clear reference to this in Peter's first preaching, when the Holy Spirit moved him to speak at Pentecost:

> Peter said to them, 'Repent, and be baptized every one of you in the name of Jesus Christ so that your sins may be forgiven; and you will receive the gift of the Holy Spirit. For the promise is for you, for your children, and for all who are far away, everyone whom the Lord our God calls to him.' (Acts 2:38-39)

With their sins forgiven those newly baptised are seen to enter fully into the life of the Christian community, including full participation in the Eucharist: 'They devoted themselves to the apostles' teaching and fellowship, to the breaking of bread and the prayers' (Acts 2:42).

The magnanimity of baptism can easily be overlooked. While it would have been a joy to welcome into the community other members of the family or pious seekers of God who had been converted, it would have been very difficult to integrate converts whose lives had previously been notorious. While there are several such persons mentioned in the Gospels, perhaps the best example is Paul himself. It seemed incredible to believers that their tormentor and persecutor had now joined them. While they would be right in thinking the news a perverse joke or, more sinisterly, an attempt at infiltration by the enemy camp, they were suspicious and afraid (Acts 9:1-31). Yet in baptism Paul's sins were forgiven, and he went on to be one of the greatest of Christian teachers and writers.

Ongoing reconciliation

The first generations of believers had one more surprise coming to them. As we saw in the first chapter, they were overwhelmed with the experience of forgiveness. They spoke as though they had been 'saved' or even 'ransomed' and most certainly 'reconciled', yet one thing continued to disrupt their peace. While Christ had vanquished death, they still could not avoid falling into sin. All wrestled with the fact that they continued to do the wrong thing, as described by Paul: 'I do not understand my own actions. For I do not do what I want, but I do the very thing I hate' (Rom 7:15). Members of the community, from the greatest to the least, continued to commit sins great and small. Both of Jesus' closest apostles, Peter and Judas, had failed him. Later on, Peter's leadership was not always inspiring and rather too human (Gal 2:11-14). Paul himself wrote often of his own struggle with sinfulness; he could not always contain his temper (Gal 5:12). Christian communities were prone to division (Gal 1:6-10; 1 Cor 1:10-17), contained factions that ganged up on the poor and left them hungry at the Lord's Supper (1 Cor 11:17-34), and followed false teachers (2 Cor 11:1-15). With more than slight exaggeration Paul upbraided the Corinthians for their inability to come to deal with sinful behaviour: 'It is actually reported that there is sexual immorality among you, and of a kind that is not found even among pagans' (1 Cor 5:1).

The first communities brought several approaches to bear on sinful behaviour in the community. And these showed both their awareness of the communal dimension of sin and the role of the body of Christ in bringing reconciliation. A person who had done something significantly wrong was neither left alone nor simply abandoned.

Confession of sin

In his letter, James recommends a first approach, namely, that Christians confess their sins to one another: 'Therefore confess your sins to one another, and pray for one another, so that you may be healed' (Jas 5:16). In this sentence he also adds a second approach: prayer for one another.

Prayer on behalf of a sinner

James is not the only witness to advocate prayer for the sinner as a way of working with God to bring God's forgiveness to bear. We see this in the first letter of John: 'If you see your brother or sister committing what is not a mortal sin, you will ask, and God will give life to such a one – to those whose sin is not mortal' (1 John 5:16). However it is James who gives us the reason that, in God's eyes, the prayer of the righteous is efficacious. Indeed, prayer made in Christ, the basis of all Christian understanding of what it is to be righteous, is authentic prayer. This is why James can add: 'The prayer of the righteous is powerful and effective' (Jas 5:16).

A gentle, personal reminder

A third strategy used by the early communities to address sinful behaviour was for a member of the community to speak to an offender, not necessarily with the knowledge or agreement of other members of the community. Such a strategy presumes some discretion, and does not give tacit permission for sin to be trumpeted about the place. Paul urges a gentle approach: 'My friends, if anyone is detected in a transgression, you who have received the Spirit should restore such a one in a spirit of gentleness' (Gal 6:1). Note too that Paul's use of the term 'transgression' reminds the community that the offences in question must be serious. At the same time he is aware that the ministry of reconciliation can provide an opening for the community itself to fall into sin: 'Take care that you yourselves are not tempted' (Gal 6:1). Paul goes on then to outline three features of an act of reconciliation: a history of serious transgression, a response by way of admonition in the spirit of gentleness, and a recognition that the community has the potential, unfortunately, to abuse the sinner. The same admonition to gentleness is found in the second letter to Timothy: 'And the Lord's servant must not be quarrelsome but kindly to everyone, an apt teacher, patient, correcting opponents with gentleness' (2 Tim 2:24-25).

A gentle but firm reproach

A variant of this approach, to be used when the offender did not listen to a lone voice, was for a small group to speak to him or her: 'If you are not listened to, take one or two others along with you, so that every word may be confirmed by the evidence of two or three witnesses' (Matt 18:16). If this too failed then the offence was to be made more public, again in the hope of bringing the offender to their senses and of being reconciled with them: 'If the member refuses to listen to them, tell it to the church' (Matt 18:17).

Community-sanctioned exclusion

What happened though if gentle admonition or a group discussion did not sway the offender to repentance? In such cases a more resolute, fourth approach was developed:

the wrongdoer was to be banished from the community: 'And if the offender refuses to listen even to the church, let such a one be to you as a Gentile and a tax collector' (Matt 18:17). Paul urged the Corinthians to do this to one of their own members whose immoral behaviour they had tolerated: 'And you are arrogant! Should you not rather have mourned, so that he who has done this would have been removed from among you?' (1 Cor 5:2). Yet the aim was reconciliation, and the exclusion was designed to prepare the way for conversion. We see this in another letter of Paul, again to the Corinthians, where he pleads for the community to lift their ban on a man they had cast out and who is now showing remorse:

> This punishment by the majority is enough for such a person; so now instead you should forgive and console him, so that he may not be overwhelmed by excessive sorrow. So I urge you to reaffirm your love for him (2 Cor 2:6-8).

Paul points out to the Corinthians that they should act out of love only. The sinner is to be loved, especially when he is outside the community. This is quite a challenge since public sin would cause confusion, division and hurt within the body of Christ, and there is a sense in which expulsion is also designed to protect the integrity of the community. Nevertheless it is the welfare of the sinner that comes first.

This reflects faith in the breadth of the reconciliation that Jesus brought; no sin is beyond his saving grace. The set of parables about the lost sheep, the lost coin and the forgiving father (Luke 15) show us how much care the community devoted to the welfare and reconciliation of sinners. In the letter of James the return of a sinner by a member of the community was understood to remit the effects of judgment and bring peace to the community:

My brothers and sisters, if anyone among you wanders from the truth and is brought back by another, you should know that whoever brings back a sinner from wandering will save the sinner's soul from death and will cover a multitude of sins (Jas 5:19-20).

Sickness and sin: anointing

Jesus was a renowned healer and, in many of the stories where he brought a person back to health, he also healed their sins. This reflected the understanding in his time that bad health and sickness, as well as accidents and plain bad luck, were seen as connected somehow to sin. The cause for the ill fortune was attributed either to the sick person themselves or to their parents, their family or their ancestors. It is no surprise then to see something of this reflected in the blessing and anointing of Christians who fall sick. Again we turn to the letter of James:

> Are any among you sick? They should call for the elders of the church and have them pray over them, anointing them with oil in the name of the Lord. The prayer of faith will save the sick, and the Lord will raise them up; and anyone who has committed sins will be forgiven (Jas 5:14-15).

Conclusion

We see in the age of the apostles that the first generations of Christians worked hard to comprehend forgiveness, sin and the reconciliation that Christ brings. They also recognised that they continued to sin, even though their sins had been wiped away in baptism and they had begun a new life. Under the inspiration of the Spirit, the community brought the forgiveness of God to everyday sin, as well as to quite serious offences, through the development of practices and rites such as confession to another member of the faithful, prayer for sinners and gentle admonition, either by an individual or a small group. They were deeply concerned about serious sin, both for the sinner and for the community itself, and developed practices of admonition, exclusion and return to bring the sinner to his or her senses, and maintain the integrity of the community.

The Scriptures give us hints that all this was not easy. The various conflicts within the church show us the communal nature of sin and how it can affect the Body of Christ. The bluntness with which the various books of the New Testament detail the shortcomings of Peter, Judas, Paul, James, the twelve and many others are telling reminders that even in leadership and power there is no refuge from sin. Sometimes communities found it difficult to identify and deal with the sins in their midst, as happened in the church of Corinth. However the communities too could find it most difficult to forgive, even when repentance seemed clear. Paul has to speak plainly to the Corinthian community for it to bring back to the fold a repentant sinner (2 Cor 2:6-8). The letter to Philemon, finally, contains a heartfelt plea for Philemon, a member of the community, to accept back the errant Onesimus because he has been such a blessing to Paul and such a help in his ministry. Forgiveness and reconciliation are not easy.

Chapter 3

Forgiveness in an Age
of Public Penance: 100-1000

This chapter deals with a span of about 900 years – quite a long stretch of time by any standards. As we move across it we will find some common elements but much that changes; it will be our task to track the differences that emerge. We will discover that some are refinements of earlier practices while others represent completely new directions. It is important to keep a keen eye both on the modifications themselves as well as on the dynamics that bring about shifts in practice. This history also throws light on our understanding of the rites and practices that we have now and on how well they are working.

Ordinary, everyday sin

We will begin our exploration of this long age with the rites that emerged to deal with ordinary, everyday sin. This matter is one of those commonly neglected in current thought, but it is an extremely important part of the lives of the faithful; it was then and it is now.

Like the first generation of Christians, the faithful knew that they commit offences which are not serious in themselves, but which mean that sin still has quite a hold over their lives and, consequently, that they are in need of forgiveness and reconciliation. For them, the practices found in the scriptures became important sources for accessing the grace of God. The baptised, then, asked God for forgiveness. As well, they understood that prayer, fasting, good works, charity and celebrating the Eucharist, including the reception of Holy Communion, were remedies for their sins. In trust they turned to a more mature Christian or to a spiritual guide and confessed their actions. They upheld the practice of praying for sinners and continued to anoint the sick with oil, seeing it as a rite that brought both physical health and spiritual wellbeing.

We can identify a range of factors operating here. One factor is that many of these approaches were private, and, in the main, entailed the sinner presenting him- or herself alone before God. Other factors were more church-based in that they involved other Christians and concerned the forms of confession and the anointing of the sick. Underneath all of these there is a deep sense of the community at work. Christians together fasted, celebrated the Eucharist, prayed for sinners and encouraged charity and almsgiving. In one sense, the sinner sought forgiveness directly from God but, in another sense, he or she did so within a Christian community environment that sought the reconciliation of sinners, trusted these various ways and actively promoted them. But from our position in history, we are inclined to see even these forms of the forgiveness of ordinary sin as involving the sinner presenting him- or herself individually before God. Yet, in an earlier age, though the sinner might be an individual, he or she never really stood 'alone'. He or she stood before God from within the church, knowing they had the direct, and indirect, support of brothers and sisters in faith.

In effect we have here church forms of devotion and piety that are the basis of a 'penitential' lifestyle. It is important to view this while bearing in mind the meaning of the word 'penitential' at that time, and not our later sense of it as referring to penalty and punishment. The Latin word *paenitentia* meant 'change of heart' or 'conversion'. In face of their everyday sin earlier faithful embraced a way of living around ongoing conversion and a deepening appreciation of the freedom and grace of their baptism.

Anointing of the sick

Anointing of the sick, though a ritual for physical healing, was also seen in this earlier age to involve the forgiveness of ordinary sins, as reflected in the letter of James (Jas 5:14-15). During this period, the rite involved prayer with the sick person and then anointing with oil that had been consecrated by the bishop. The oil could also be drunk as a way of anointing the inner parts of the body. Externally, the anointing was administered by a lay person, a priest or the bishop himself, though, eventually, around the ninth century, the administration of the oil became the preserve of the ordained. There is a sense here in which the healing of sickness and the forgiveness of sins both work to bring a deeper wholeness to the ailing person. However the forgiveness of sinners under public penance was not celebrated through anointing.

Serious sin

The forgiveness of serious sin provided enormous difficulties for the Christian community. While it was possible to provide something of a list of serious offences, such as murder, abortion, adultery and apostasy, it was not always easy to know the gravity of any particular action. Some minor actions could be done out of a deeply sinful intention, while some more major offences could be in part the result of ignorance, immaturity or weakness, as understood by St Augustine.[1] Yet some particular types of sins affected the whole community. As we saw above with Paul and his feisty Corinthians, the reintegration of someone who had committed serious sin was fraught with difficulties.

---

1. *De div quaest 83* q 26.

Baptism

The primary means for the forgiveness of serious sin was baptism. This made perfect sense in a church where, in the main, baptism was administered to adults who were responding to a call to conversion and a new way of life in Christ. In the saving waters of baptism the slate was wiped clean, sin washed away, life regenerated, and the new Christian clothed in fresh garments. It was an experience of death and rebirth.

The discipline of public penance

But what about serious sin committed after baptism? Such a challenge to the community was met with only the greatest difficulty. The main strategy for meeting it was based on the dynamic that came from the scriptures: the sinner was to be 'excluded' so as to be able to 'return'. From this developed the rites of public penance. These were quite formal and structured, since the community recognised that serious sin jeopardised the soul of the sinner and affected the community. Yet there was another part to the picture: in the background was the theological struggle over whether serious sins committed after baptism could be forgiven at all, let alone for a second time or more. It remained incomprehensible to many believers that God could be so gracious and forgiving – a factor which accounts for the harshness of the penalties and practices.

By and large the pattern for the rites of public penance had the following form. The sinner made a request to undertake a public penance to the bishop, and, at the same time, the sinner confessed his or her action to him. The bishop then set an appropriate discipline or penance. It is worth remembering that it was the penance that was public, not necessarily the prior sin. When the penance was completed the bishop reintegrated the public penitent into the community at a special rite. Often this rite was held on Holy Thursday.

What did the penitential discipline look like? Tertullian (approx. 160-225) offers the following, typically harsh, view:

> It bids him lie in sackcloth and ashes, to cover his body with filthy rags, to plunge his soul into sorrow, to exchange sin for suffering. Moreover it demands that you know only such food and drink as is plain … it means that you habitually nourish prayer by fasting, that you sigh and weep and groan day and night to the Lord your God, that you prostrate yourself at the feet of the priests and kneel before the beloved of God, making all the brethren commissioned ambassadors of your prayer for pardon.[2]

As we can see, public penance was truly public, and involved the denial of luxuries, the wearing of uncomfortable clothes that clearly indicated one's status, fasting, expressions of sorrow, and humility. Tertullian did not mention here two other common features, namely, sexual abstinence – often for the remainder of one's life – and abandoning any ambition for public office. The rite of public penance clearly did not serve an ambitious career path.

The penitent was allowed to participate in the Eucharist but only to a limited degree. In the first stages of the penitential process he or she could attend the liturgy till the end of the homily only; then the penitent had to depart. As the time of penance passed the penitent could remain for longer at communal worship, however participation in Holy Communion was forbidden until the bishop had reconciled the penitent with the church.

Penalties could last for a decade or more, with typical figures being around nine to eleven years. But pastoral considerations came into play. Penitents who were dying were readmitted to the Eucharist so that they could die in

---

2. Tertullian, *Treatises on Penance: On Penance and On Purity*, translated and annotated by William P. Le Saint (London: Longmans, Green and Co., 1959) 31.

peace amongst the community, nourished by the bread of life and the cup of salvation. There is a story of a young man who, in danger of death, entered public penance, but on recovery wished to marry. In these circumstances the bishop lifted the stricture against lifelong sexual abstinence. However this softening depended upon the pastoral understanding of the particular bishop. In contrast, there was a pastoral motivation in the opposite direction that saw any softening as weakening the fabric of reconciliation and maintained that harshness was a better deterrent against serious sin and closer to the mind of God.

The authority to pronounce the forgiveness of sin

We can already see some interesting responses to the question of who in the community has responsibility for pronouncing that a person has been forgiven his or her sin. In ordinary, everyday sin forgiveness was not mediated by a particular person but, rather, by the community, through its teaching its members that a range of acts done in good faith showed that forgiveness had been applied to the sinner. The community, then, prized almsgiving, prayer, acts of charity, participation in the Eucharist and receiving Holy Communion, confessing to a holy person and the like. The authority of these actions was based on the experience of a living church community which understood the value and power in these practices. The forgiveness of serious sin in baptism had much the same character except that, in baptism, it was the rite itself that underscored the forgiveness. Authority here was vested in the sacramental nature of the ritual.

The rites of public penance, and indeed the rites for the hearing and forgiveness of grave sin, all pointed to the pivotal role of the bishop as head of the church and the key figure in bringing the forgiveness of Christ to the sinner. The power to mediate God's forgiveness was here based in authority figures in church structure. Yet this was not the complete story. Could a person of impeccable holiness also forgive a public sinner, even against the will of the bishop? The early Christians knew that the bishop was not the only authority and that there was an authentic power and innate Godly authority resting in other members of the Body of Christ. In particular, sinners sought the intercession of Christians who were imprisoned and awaiting martyrdom. The key here is that, upon their gruesome death, martyrs were understood to sit beside the judgment seat of God and so to have extraordinary powers of intercession. What followed was the practice of public sinners seeking out Christians who were about to be martyred; these were known as 'confessors'. Once a confessor of the faith was convinced the sinner's conversion and repentance was authentic, he or she would write a letter to the bishop urging mercy. In writing the letter, the martyr-to-be promised to pray for the sinner before God – a virtual guarantee of forgiveness. This left the bishop in a terrible quandary as to whether he would be more harsh and unremitting than God. The historian Eusebius (260-340) recounts the words of Bishop Dionysius on this dilemma:

> What must we do? Shall we be of the same opinion and of the same mind as they [the confessors], and shall we observe their decision and charity and be merciful to those who they pitied, or shall we hold their decision unjust, and establish ourselves as judges of their opinions, and cause grief to goodness, and to overturn their order?[3]

In sum we can see that the authority to bring forgiveness to bear on sin rested in different ways in the Body of Christ. It was vested in the living practices of the community, the sacramental rites of baptism and anointing of the sick, the

---

3. Eusebius, *Ecclesiastical History (Bks 6-10)*, The Fathers of the Church Vol. 29, translated by Roy J. Defarrari, (New York: Fathers of the Church, Inc., 1965), 77.

authority of the bishop, and, in some cases, the holiness of members of Christ's Body.

The eventual toll of public penance

Difficulties with the system of public penance became more obvious as the place of the church in society changed. By the fifth century the church was no longer a group of relatively small communities under intermittent persecution keen to maintain their identity and faith. Rather, Christians had become actively engaged in the world, in politics, business and the military. They came from all levels of society. Public discipline no longer fitted such an environment or culture and so fewer and fewer people were able to make use of it. Clearly anyone who took up public penance was closed off from career, family life and an early return to normal living in the community.

The church too, by this time, had some centuries of experience behind it and had dealt painfully with difficult questions. During the time of the persecutions, in the second and third centuries, many people had denounced their faith, only to regret this when the pressure was off; and some people denounced it more than once. Communities were in a quandary deciding what to do with such people. There was a growing sense that public penance was neither a successful deterrent to serious sin nor that it always suited the need to reconcile sinners.

This ritual form also began to have a deleterious effect on the life of the church itself. For ordinary believers, it so strongly reinforced the fear of falling into grave sin that parents held their children back from baptism when they were young in case they committed grave sin in their youth or early adult life. Baptism, then, was put off until later in life. We can get another glimpse here of why the early Christians found the story of how Jesus forgave the woman caught in adultery so difficult.

The rites of public penance remained in the ritual books of the church and were faithfully copied by successive generations of copyists but were called on less and less. While the rites nevertheless did not die out, they remained a once-in-a-lifetime opportunity for the forgiveness of scandalous, grave, public sin. In practice, however, by the tenth century, they were more a relic of the past than a living practice.

A penitential spirituality

Yet public penance did live on, though in a different form. It gave rise to a form of public penitential spirituality. Christians began to see this form as an ideal way to review one's life, especially when embraced for a short period of time, such as Lent. Lay folk would take up the discipline of public penance as a form of preparation for death, allowing them to make amends for any harm they had brought about during the course of their lives. As this practice developed, 'penitents' would commence the discipline on the first day of Lent by covering themselves with ashes – the origin of Ash Wednesday – and then they would receive reconciliation on Holy Thursday.

Conclusion

The church of the first millennium had a range of strategies and rites to convey the reconciliation that God has brought about directly into the lives of the faithful. All these rites and practices operated within the context of the Christian community, even the seemingly most private and individual ones. They show the struggle church communities had in dealing with serious sin, and how practices suitable in one era can have damaging effects in other times and contexts. While this early period is usually characterised as one of public penance, this rite was however celebrated in the context of other rites, practices and spiritualities of conversion and reconciliation.

Chapter 4

Forgiveness in an Age of Private Penance: 1000 to the Present

In this chapter we will focus on developments in rites of private penance. In effect, we will chart the rise, and various understandings, of what we have come to call 'confession'. Be warned, however. We must be careful not to read our current views, presuppositions and practices back into earlier periods too closely. We need especially to be aware of the deep anxiety in Christians in this age because of their feeling that they were in constant danger of falling into mortal sin. While this should be part of the spiritual understanding of all the baptised, during much of this long period it seemed as if grave sin was almost an everyday peril.

While the focus here will be on the forms of individual confession, we should not lose sight of other practices that have been part of the times. The sacraments of baptism and the anointing of the sick continued to be held to forgive sins, and the ordinary, everyday means of fasting, prayer, almsgiving and the like continued to be applied to the forgiveness of sin. Early in this period, the communal form of entering public penance during Lent was still in place. As well during this period, pilgrimage emerged as an important remedy for major sin, and general absolution was administered in a variety of circumstances. On major feast days, when a large number of the faithful wished to receive Holy Communion, a rite of general absolution could be inserted into Mass. Throughout this period too we see the emergence of a range of penitential movements and groups.

Individual confession to a fellow sinner

As the church gained hold in Ireland it developed practices that were different from those in Rome. This was in part because the Irish were converted by monks and so took up monastic customs, such as confessing sins to a holy person, whether male or female. A sinner, feeling guilt for his or her sin, would confess to such a spiritual guide, be given a penalty, and, finally would be offered a form of absolution when the penalty was completed. This penalty could be shortened if an acceptable alternative could be found.

Later Irish missionary monks returned to evangelise Europe and brought with them this innovative practice. It met stiff resistance from church officials. It was attacked because it was thought to be too individualistic and lacking in a strong sense of the involvement of the community. Further it was deemed as lax because it allowed for major sins such as adultery to be forgiven on their repitition. It was also attacked because it was inconsistent: different confessors could give different penalties for the same type of sin. Nevertheless the faithful, especially those in the Germanic regions of Europe, accepted it as a welcome form to receive the forgiveness of God. Eventually it became the norm to make confession to a priest or, in some cases, to a deacon. It also became clear that it was impractical to have absolution after the penance was completed, so the order of these two elements was reversed.

What did the liturgy look like? We have a rite in the collection of Haltigar (d. 830) which portrays a layered, prayerful liturgy.[1] First, the Christian seeking forgiveness

---

1. See James Dallen, *The Reconciling Community: The Rite of Penance* (New York: Pueblo Publishing Company, 1986) 114.

approached the confessor, usually a priest. Then confessor and priest fasted together for a day, this being followed by the actual confession of sin. Next the confessor went aside to pray, seeking God's mercy and assistance for himself and the sinner. Following this the priest gave advice to the sinner and assigned the penance by which the sins were redeemed. Psalms were prayed and intercessions made petitioning God's mercy. To bring the rite to a close the minister imposed his hand and made a further prayer for forgiveness. The logical time for this sort of rite to take place was at the beginning of Lent, with the penitent returning for solemn reconciliation in Holy Week. The confessor expected a stipend for hearing the confession and imposing a penance.

We can see then that this was a serious liturgy of forgiveness of grave sin. The novelty was that it was done in private rather than publicly. However it was a rite within the church, and it came to require an official minister, lending something of a communal character to an otherwise closed set of proceedings. As well, both penitent and priest recognised their own sinfulness and need for prayer throughout the ritual.

The importance of contrition

The key element in the first understanding of private confession was contrition. If penitents were not truly sorry for their sins, then they had no reason or compulsion to take part in this liturgical rite. It was sorrow for sin, and the desire to be at peace, that strengthened the will of the sinner to confess, undertake penance, and receive absolution. In this sense, the focus of the ritual was on the penitent and his or her conversion of heart, with contrition the element that gave integrity to the confession of sin.

The link between confession of sins and receiving Holy Communion

By the turn of the first millennium the reception of Holy Communion by the faithful had become a rare event. Eventually laws were decreed to address the situation, with all of the members of the community required to receive Holy Communion once a year, usually at Easter. The parish priest would keep a list of all who had come forward and so was in a position to admonish anyone who had not taken Communion during the preceding year. This had an effect on the rite of confession because parallel laws were set in place that obliged the faithful to confess once a year as well, in preparation for receiving Communion. We see this link between confession of sins and receiving Holy Communion most clearly in the decrees of the Fourth Lateran Council (1215), which also taught that confession must be to the parish priest:

> All the faithful of either sex, after they have reached the age of discernment, should individually confess all their sins in a faithful manner to their own priest at least once a year, and let them take care to do what they can to perform the penance imposed on them … if any persons wish to confess their sin to another priest let them first ask and obtain the permission of their own priest; for otherwise the other priest will not have the power to absolve or bind them.[2]

Four points here are worth highlighting. One is the creation of a clear link between private confession and Communion. While the document from the council presumes the confession of serious sin, it must be remembered that in this quite pessimistic age many thought that it was very easy to fall into mortal sin. Nevertheless we end up with a strange and somewhat ironic situation. In Christian tradition the reception of

---

2. Fourth Lateran Council, 21, *On Confession being made, and not revealed by the priest, and on communicating at least at Easter*.

Communion had been seen as a means of the forgiveness of sins. Now, with participation in Communion a rare event, a member of the faithful needed his or her sins forgiven before they could receive the sacrament of forgiveness!

The second point is that the penitent was to confess to his or her parish priest. While this may seem to us an unnecessary hindrance, it reflects a strong pastoral instinct. It was the parish priest who had pastoral responsibility for penitents, and so they were in the best position to understand the sinner's contrition and to convey healing and forgiveness.

The third point is that the decree radically changed the nature of private confession. It was no longer a free act but a compulsory one; every baptised person was affected. Again this highlighted pessimism about sin, reinforcing the view that all human beings are constantly in danger of grave sin. As well, the 'sinner' could no longer choose the person to whom he or she would confess, compromising the freedom of the sinner to take part in the rite. With freedom compromised, it was more likely that the participants were less candid about their sins and more forced in espousing their contrition.

The final point flows from the first three. As the rite of private confession became more and more central the other methods for the forgiveness of sins, such as Eucharist and Communion, fasting, almsgiving and prayer, lost currency. Devotions developed that concentrated on how sinful and in need of penance the faithful were rather than on celebrating the forgiveness and reconciliation that Jesus had brought.

The priest as judge

This inability to read how contrite a person was, allied with changes in the theology about the power of the ordained, led to a change in understanding of the rite of individual confession. A new approach emerged from the application of legal and courtroom language to the sacrament. It was easy enough to view the sinner as a 'criminal' since he or she had broken God's law. Correspondingly, the priest came to be viewed, not so much as a fellow sinner, but as a judge. Soon the contrition of the sinner came to be seen as important but secondary. Rather, the key was in the absolution from the priest, who, as judge, could pronounce forgiveness. Consequently the penance that the priest gave was understood as part pastoral healing and part criminal sentence. This had an effect on the way the sacrament was celebrated. Previously the confessor had wanted to know about the state of the penitent's heart, as he helped discern with a sinner the depth of contrition and so potential for conversion. With this new development it became important for the priest to interrogate sinners about their sin rather than their sorrow, since he needed to know the exact way in which divine law had been broken and then fix an appropriate punishment. In effect the rite of private confession became a ritual centred around the priest, his authority to question the penitent and his power to absolve, with contrition underplayed and the role of the penitent in the rite diminished.

Conclusion

This chapter brings us out of the past right to the present day. The four basic elements of our contemporary practice are in place: confession of sins, contrition, the completion of a penance, and absolution. We have named the main features in the development of private confession, including the movement to confession to a priest and the change of emphasis from contrition to absolution. We have also noted how approaches to the sacrament related to the understanding of sin at the time. The laws that made annual confession compulsory also left a lasting mark on our practice and spirituality of reconciliation. Much devotional practice aimed at seeking forgiveness for sins rather than at celebrating the grace already given.

Chapter 5

An Overview of Current Rites and Devotions

When asked about the current ritual forms for the reconciliation of sins many Catholics immediately think of going to confession, or, more accurately the *Rite of Penance*. Yet, history has shown us that these forms are not the only ritual forms for the forgiveness of sins. Like all sacraments, the *Rite of Penance* is set within a context of other sacramental rites and effective devotional practices. In this chapter we will concentrate on these forms and then, in chapter six, we will examine the *Rite of Penance* itself. Because we are dealing with the contemporary situation, there will be a number of references to the renewed rites that have emerged from the Second Vatican Council (1962-65). However, to show the long-standing importance of some devotional practices we will include references to the Council of Trent (1545-63).

Baptism

The opening paragraph of the General Introduction to our *Rite of Christian Initiation of Adults* sets out the three pillars of initiation as freedom from sin, adoption in the Spirit as God's children, and participation in the Eucharist:

> In the sacraments of Christian initiation we are freed from the power of darkness and joined to Christ's death, burial and resurrection. We receive the Spirit of filial adoption

and are part of the entire people of God in the celebration of the memorial of Christ's death and resurrection.[1]

The Introduction gives further emphasis to this freedom from sin: 'Baptism, the cleansing with water by the power of the living word, washes away every stain of sin, original and personal.'[2]

Anointing of the sick

The sacrament of the anointing of the sick remains associated with the forgiveness of sins, as it has been from the time of the New Testament (Jas 5:14-15). The current rite of anointing echoes this. The apostolic constitution from Paul VI which established the rite contains a quotation from the Council of Trent: 'This reality is in fact the grace of the Holy Spirit, whose anointing takes away sins, if any still remain, and the remnants of sin.'[3] The current Vatican II rite maintains that the forgiveness of sins belongs to the ritual: 'If necessary, the sacrament also provides the sick person with the forgiveness of sins, and the completion of Christian penance.'[4] It is not too surprising that there is some dispute as to how the sacrament is related to the forgiveness of grave sins and whether there is a need for subsequent integral confession. Nevertheless we can see that the anointing of the sick is a sacrament of forgiveness.

Eucharist

As remarked earlier, an often overlooked teaching is that Christian tradition has associated the celebration of the Eucharist with the forgiveness of sins. Over four hundred

1. *Rite of Christian Initiation of Adults*, General Introduction, n. 1.
2. *Rite of Christian Initiation of Adults*, General Introduction, n. 5.
3. Paul VI, apostolic constitution *Sacram Unctionem Infirmorum* (30 November 1972), in *The Rites of the Catholic Church*, Vol. 1, 772. For the Council of Trent reference, see The Council of Trent, Session 14, ch. 2.
4. *Rite of Anointing of the Sick*, General Introduction, n. 6.

and fifty years ago the Council of Trent was most insistent on this, even for the forgiveness of grave sin:

> Hence the holy council teaches that this is a truly propitiatory sacrifice, and brings it about that if we approach God with sincere hearts and upright faith, and with awe and reverence, 'we receive mercy and find grace to help in time of need' (Heb 4:16). For the Lord is appeased by this offering, he gives the gracious gift of repentance; he absolves even enormous offences and sins.[5]

The document does not develop how the celebration of the Eucharist is applied to grave sin. Yet we can see that a strong connection is drawn between the memorial of the reconciliation of all things in Christ and the forgiveness of our sins.

More commonly, the Eucharist is spoken of in relation to the forgiveness of sins that fall under the category of 'venial', a matter that the Council of Trent also addressed. It taught that communion was both spiritual food and a remedy for everyday sin:

> [Christ] wished this sacrament to be taken as the spiritual food of souls, to nourish and strengthen them as they live by his life who said: 'He who eats Me will live because of Me' (Jn 6:57); and as an antidote to free us from daily faults and to preserve us from mortal sin.[6]

Consequently the Council of Trent encouraged frequent communion:

> [Christians] should believe and reverence these sacred mysteries of his body and blood with such constancy and firmness of faith, such dedication of mind, such devotion and worship, that they may be able to receive frequently that life supporting bread, and that it may be for them truly the life of the soul and the unending health of mind.[7]

---

5. The Council of Trent, Session 22, ch. 2.
6. The Council of Trent, Session 13, ch. 2.
7. The Council of Trent, Session 13, ch. 8.

As well, the council decreed confession be made before Communion for those whose consciences were burdened with mortal sin:

> The practice of the church declares that examination necessary, so that no one who is aware of personal mortal sin, however contrite he may feel, should approach the holy eucharist without first having made a sacramental confession.[8]

Devotional practices

In understanding Communion as a remedy for everyday sin, the Council of Trent did no more than reiterate the common heritage of the church. Trent numbered 'devotional' confession amongst the many practices for the forgiveness of everyday sins:

> For venial sins, by which we are not cut off from the grace of God and into which we more frequently fall, although they may be admitted in confession (as the practice of devout persons shows), can nevertheless be passed over in silence without fault, and expiated by many other remedies.[9]

The other remedies Trent included were: Sunday Eucharist with Communion, prayer, fasting, confession of sins to a holy person, and almsgiving. These devotional practices remain as part of Christian life today, and offer balance to any overuse of the sacramental rites.

Conclusion

Reconciliation is at the heart of the gospel. It is no surprise that we have such a variety of sacraments and devotional practices to enable the faithful to take up the reconciliation and forgiveness that God has brought to us through Christ. This range allows the Spirit to move within us in as broad a manner as possible to bring us to conversion and into communion with God. In light of these sacraments and devotions we now turn to examine the *Rite of Penance* itself.

---

8. The Council of Trent, Session 13, ch. 7.
9. The Council of Trent, Session 14, ch. 5.

Chapter 6

The *Rite of Penance*

The *Rite of Penance* takes its place amongst the sacraments and devotional forms discussed in the previous chapter. This helps us realise that it does not carry the entire burden of ritualising reconciliation since, too often, we restrict our understanding of the forgiveness of sins to the celebration of the *Rite of Penance*, and, even more narrowly, to individual confession. In this chapter we will examine the *Rite of Penance* and open up some of the implications for celebrating the rite.

It is important to note that the *Rite of Penance* actually contains four rites. The more familiar three, the 'Rite of Reconciliation of Individual Penitents' (the 'first' rite), the 'Rite of Reconciliation of Several Penitents with Individual Confession and Absolution' (the communal 'second' rite), and the 'Rite of Reconciliation of Several Penitents with General Confession and Absolution' (the 'third' rite), are complemented by non-sacramental Penitential Services (*Rite of Penance*, Appendix 2 – the 'fourth' rite). These latter celebrations are official rites of the church and deserve their due.

Further, it is worth recalling the five foundations upon which these rites are built. Each rite is based around four acts: contrition in the sinner, confession of his or her sins, acts of penance and satisfaction, and absolution. The fifth foundation is that these are encompassed within the actions of the Word of God in our hearts, lives and communities.

Reconciliation as a ritual event

The first thing we need to be aware of is that we are dealing with an act of worship. In this we are reminded of the teachings of the Constitution on the Sacred Liturgy (*Sacrosanctum Concilium*) that, in our celebration of the rites, there ought be full, active and conscious participation in ritual:

> Pastors of souls must, therefore, realize that, when the liturgy is celebrated, something more is required than the mere observation of the laws governing valid and licit celebration; it is their duty also to ensure that the faithful take part fully aware of what they are doing, actively engaged in the rite, and enriched by its effects.[1]

As clear as this quality of participation is in the three communal forms, it also applies to the 'first' rite. There, both participants, the penitent and the priest, have parts to play. Neither is above or over the rite. The prayers or responses of neither ought be diminished. We could well ask whether our recent practice has taken into account that more is required than the mere adherence to the laws governing valid and licit celebration.

The shape of the rites

Our practice ought to be attentive to the shape of these four rites. Somewhat surprisingly, given the controversies that rage round them, they follow a common format. When compared, the main parts become clear; see table 1, opposite.

---

1. *Sacrosanctum Concilium*, n. 11. See also n. 14.

Range of ritual elements	Occurrence of ritual elements according to specific rite			
	'1st'	'2nd'	'3rd'	'4th'
Greeting	✓	✓	✓	✓
Reading from the Word of God	optional	✓	✓	✓
Contrition/ Examination of Conscience/ General confession of sins	before rite	✓	✓	✓
Integral confession of sins	✓	✓	after rite	
Suitable counsel	✓ to penitent	✓ to penitent	✓ in homily	✓ in homily
Penance/ satisfaction	✓ to penitent	✓ to penitent	✓ in homily	
Prayer of contrition	✓ by penitent	✓ by penitent	✓ in homily	✓ by penitent
Absolution	✓	✓	✓	✓
Proclamation of praise	✓	✓	✓	✓
Dismissal	✓	✓	✓	✓

Table 1. The range of ritual elements in the various rites of reconciliation and their occurrence in specific rites.

Within the celebration of a rite of reconciliation, there are four movements of inner conversion. *Contrition* signifies heartfelt sorrow and aversion for sin committed. *Confession* is the act of those who in their heart openly acknowledge sin and fault in the face of God's mercy. *Penance* or *satisfaction* is undertaken as a remedy for the effects of sins committed and a help to renewal of life. Finally, *absolution*, a sign of God's pardon, brings the rite to completion and offers penitents' hearts the healing experience of complete forgiveness.

A number of points are worth noting. One is that the rites take into consideration the variety of meanings of 'confession'. Participation in the rite itself, and especially acknowledgement of the word of God, manifest a primary meaning of confession: the confession of *faith*. The proclamation of praise that comes at the conclusion of the rite gives voice to a second meaning of Christian confession: the confession of *praise*. The third meaning, the one which appears to be uppermost in our current practice, is the confession of *sins*. This third confession ritually takes place within the context of faith and praise.

A second point to note is the importance of the Word of God in the rite. It is highly recommended as a part of the rite of individual confession, and it is central in the three communal rites. Moreover, the ritual book devotes a considerable amount of space to the provision of a selection of suitable Scripture passages. The 'first' rite has a dozen passages assigned to it. Another section contains a hundred suitable passages for the rite of reconciliation of several penitents. These, and others, are also available for the individual rite. The importance of these passages cannot be underestimated since it is the word of God that calls us to conversion. Without hearing a selection from the Scriptures there is the possibility that the 'word' of the minister can tend to predominate in the 'first' rite, rather than the divine words.

A final point concerns the question of how priest and penitents each see themselves in the rite. What difference does it bring if the priest sees himself first as a presider? What difference does it make if penitents see themselves first as active participants? Before we look more closely at this matter, however, we need to ask who are intended to be participants in the rite.

The intended participants in the rite

As we have seen from the Council of Trent, the sacramental rites of penance are intended for the reconciliation of those in grave sin. This is the reason for confession being integral. All grave sins are to be confessed, allowing the priest to make a fitting judgment and to apply an appropriate remedy.

At the same time, the 'first' rite is often encouraged in many quarters for its spiritual and devotional benefits. Contemporary church documents place both conciliatory and devotional intentions together without attending to their different purposes. We have to be very careful here. The original role of the 'first' rite for the forgiveness of grave sin can appear to be secondary to the potential of individual confession to bring spiritual progress. We need to be cautious because the rite of individual confession is not designed specifically for this type of pastoral care.

In fact, new questions emerge. For instance: what is the role of the priest in 'devotional' confession? And how well does this fit in with the ritual structure? There is also the question of what type of confession a penitent needs to make, especially if integral confession is not a requirement unless grave sin is involved. In terms of the ritual, there is a need to know what aspects of the rite enable spiritual progress, and how these can be enhanced. A 'devotional' confession should make more use of the Scripture reading, allowing the widest application of the Word of God to the life of the penitent and priest alike as an avenue for assisting spiritual progress. Further, we can ask how this devotional form sits alongside the more traditional forms, which Trent describes as 'many other remedies'. It would be a great pity if the rite of individual confession, designed to deal with grave sin, replaced the traditional forms and pieties that the baptised have used through the centuries to realise that God has forgiven their sins.

The rite of individual confession was developed to deal with a particular situation, namely, a person in grave sin. However, we can see that it is available to be used for another purpose, when entered into as a rite for gaining spiritual advice and reassurance. This can leave priest and people alike a bit confused about the rite and how it can help them. As well, it can leave pastors and faithful closed to all the other avenues available in the tradition for the forgiveness of everyday sin.

In the midst of this variety, we still need to ask how both priest and people understand themselves when taking part in this act of worship.

The priest's roles in the rites

There are five ways by which the priest can be understood in the rite. The ordained minister is the *representative* of the reconciling church, the sacrament of Christ on earth. The role is described in biblical terms: 'He reveals the heart of the Father and reflects the image of Christ the Good Shepherd'.[2] Moreover, the priest is the *presider* of this rite and, consequently, should lead it so that this liturgy is an action of grace, ever mindful that it is Christ who leads our worship. As confessor, the sacred minister takes up roles as *judge*, *healer*, and *counsellor*. It was the role as judge, and the juridical understanding of the sacrament, that undergirded the thinking of the Council of Trent. This

---

2. *Rite of Penance*, Introduction, n. 10.

combination continues to influence the current theology and practice of ministers and penitents alike. This paradigm is at its most unsatisfactory when it fails to appreciate that all models based on court procedures and disciplines fall under, and are themselves judged by, the saving ministry of Christ. Though the priest may take up a role as Christ, yet the ordained presider is not Christ. One of the important insights of the penitential practices of the first millennium is that the celebrant of the rite of penance is a *fellow sinner*. Priests especially are mindful when they hear a confession that they have been privileged to enter a moment of grace, openness and compassion. Finally, as both believer and sinner, the priest is truly a *confessor* of faith in God and of praise for what has been done in Christ through the power of the Spirit.

Penitents' roles in the rites

It should not surprise us that there is a close parallel between the minister and penitents in the ritual form. Firstly, penitents too represent the church. They exemplify its continual need for conversion: 'The Church, which includes within itself sinners and is at the same time holy and always in need of purification, constantly pursues repentance and renewal.'[3] As we are dealing with liturgy, penitents are participants in ritual. Their involvement necessitates the full, conscious and active participation which characterises the liturgy emerging from the reforms of the Second Vatican Council. As the priest is the confessor, so the penitents are seekers of reconciliation and healing. It goes without saying then that, like the ordained minister, they acknowledge they are sinners. Finally, as participants in the rite of penance, penitents are confessors. They confess their faith in the loving, merciful God. They confess their praise for the mighty works of God in Christ through the

---

3. *Rite of Penance*, Introduction, n. 3.

Spirit. They confess their sin and their sinfulness. Table 2 compares the roles of priest and of penitents in the rites of reconciliation.

Ordained Minister	Penitents
Represents the reconciling church, the sacrament of Christ on earth.	Represent the church, exemplifying its continual need for conversion.
Presides over the chosen rite, sensitive to liturgy as an action of grace under the ultimate leadership of Christ.	Participate fully, consciously and actively in the chosen rite.
Exercises roles of judge, healer and counsellor within the saving ministry of Christ.	Seek reconciliation and healing.
Acknowledges himself implicitly to be a fellow sinner.	Acknowledge themselves explicitly to be sinners.
Confesses faith in God and praise for what has been done in Christ, through the power of the Spirit.	Confess their: • faith in the loving, merciful God; • praise for the mighty works of God in Christ through the Spirit • sins and sinfulness.

Table 2. Parallels between the roles of the ordained minister and those of penitents in the rites of reconciliation.

Conclusion

Reflecting on the ritual nature of the sacrament of penance opens up its richness and potential. As well, it casts light on some of the present-day confusions. The similarity of structure between all four ritual forms should alert us to their commonality rather than to just their differences. At the heart of each of these liturgies is a celebration of contrition, confession, penance and absolution, framed by the actions of the Word of God. Precisely as liturgies they require the full, conscious and active participation of priest and faithful alike. There is some confusion in the encouragement of the use of the rite of individual reconciliation as a form of assistance to spiritual growth. An overemphasis on the practice of 'devotional' confession can serve to underplay the other devotional forms discussed in the previous chapter and to recast the non-sacramental rite as something second rate.

Chapter 7

Wisdom Offered
and Received

The practices of forgiveness within the body of Christ across the centuries show that the church has a 'wisdom' about reconciliation to share with broader society and culture. At the same time, this history shows how rites of forgiveness have had to adapt to changes in context, meaning that the church is always in a position to receive wisdom as it attempts to remain true to the ever extending depth and reach of the salvation brought by Christ. In this chapter, then, we discuss the ecumenical possibilities of our study as well as the contribution our rites can make to broader movements for reconciliation.

Ecumenical possibilities

From the time of the Protestant Reformation (1500s) to the present there has been considerable discomfort in Protestant circles with the Catholic practice of confession to a priest. Typically the response from members of the Churches of the Reformation is that all that is necessary is for the sinner to turn in faith to God through an act of authentic sorrow to enable God's comforting love to bring forgiveness. The grounds of the unease with sacramental confession to a priest have been enflamed by the bitter polemics that have accompanied the Reformation and its Catholic response. It is time to revisit this situation, especially in light of the history and practices we have discussed in the previous chapters.

First, we can see that Catholic practice has been broader than many Christians, Catholic and Protestant alike, have understood. There is common ground in that all Churches can affirm the multiple ways in which we are able to take up the forgiveness and reconciliation that God has granted us through Christ.

Secondly, we can see that the practice of reconciliation has been modified across history in response to the changes in the way cultures and nations and times have understood sin, grace and the place of the church in society. With this in mind we can explore whether in the Reformation there emerged other ways of thinking about conversion and ritual that in turn affected practices of reconciliation. In particular, Martin Luther (1483-1546), the towering figure of the Reformation, put words to a different view of what it was to be a sinner and to repent. The experience he enunciated was one of the complete hopelessness of the sinner before temptation. It was a strong reading of a passage from Paul's letter to the Romans:

> I do not understand my own actions. For I do not do what I want, but I do the very thing I hate ... But in fact it is no longer I that do it, but sin that dwells within me ... Wretched man that I am! Who will rescue me from this body of death? Thanks be to God through Jesus Christ our Lord! (excerpts from Rom 7:15-25).

In light of this insight Martin Luther found penitential practices to be extremely unhelpful because they only made him feel more helpless and wretched. His theological stance was that human beings are so sinful because of their broken human nature that ongoing conversion was impossible. The only answer was a radical act of faith through Christ in the grace of God, a mercy that God has freely and unconditionally chosen to bestow. In hindsight it is clear that this different view of sin required a different ritual approach. What is also clear is that here neither processes of ongoing conversion nor even ritual itself could be trusted since anything that involved human beings was necessarily tainted because of the implicit corrupting influence of sinful humanity. On the other hand, the Catholic understanding of sin was that humanity was wounded but still graced and hence capable of growth in holiness since it continued to contain the 'likeness' of God (cf. Gen 1:27) even after Adam and Eve were expelled from Eden. It is not hard to see why such a huge change in thinking lead to rejection of many rites and practices and to fierce polemic.

The wisdom of the history of reconciliation offers a chance to view this situation afresh. Leaving aside the misunderstandings on both sides, and the poor practices that often emerged out of pieties and devotions, both Catholic and Protestant approaches rely on the single truth that salvation has been accomplished for us in Christ, that creation has been reconciled to God, and that freedom is ours in the Holy Spirit. Yet the Reformation allowed for a second understanding of the sinfulness of humanity to come to the fore. In many ways it represents a bleak view of human nature, yet it is not without foundation – given what human beings do to each other and to the world – and it offers true hope because it has Christ firmly at its centre. The heart of this form of reconciliation is sincere contrition and confession. However, this time, the confession is directly to God, since only God and the divine Word are trustworthy. Moreover, this confession to God is usually set within a prayer context of adoration, thanksgiving and petition. The Churches that emerged from the Reformation displayed an understandable distrust of symbols and rites, given their view that all human activity is liable to be corrupted.

What wisdom can be found in all this? It is important for Catholics and Protestants to be comfortable that each has a singular emphasis in their approach to sin and conversion based on their particular interpretations of how sin has affected humanity. In effect, these different understandings require different approaches, a feature which is consistent with the history of reconciliation. As well, the hard lines of Reformation polemics have given way. This has enabled Catholics to retrieve the breadth of their tradition so that Catholic practices are not reduced to 'confession to a priest', even though this remains a vital part of the rites of reconciliation. As well, the ecumenical framework has allowed Protestants to create reconciliation services, symbols and forms that give public expression to God's reconciling grace. Moreover, our differences in practice reflect the complexity of sin and human nature, along with the need to confront the reality and effects of sin with as many approaches as possible. In this, Catholic and Protestant responses can be seen as complementary rather than as opposites, with a longer reading of history uncovering more common ground than expected.

Reconciliation movements

The Catholic wisdom around reconciliation has something to offer the movements towards reconciliation that have emerged in recent times. The public discussion and settlement of acts of aggression, violence and injustice have taken root in contemporary consciousness. Some impetus for this has come from the closure brought about by the Nuremburg trials after World War II, even though these were at heart a juridical process. More recently, however, reconciliation within societies has become an urgent priority, as seen in the South African Truth and Reconciliation Commission with their motto, 'Truth: The Road to Reconciliation'. The reconciliation process in South Africa was understood by the government and nation in the following terms: '[the] commission is a necessary exercise to enable South Africans to come to terms with their past on a morally accepted basis and to advance the cause of reconciliation'.[1] In Australia

1. *Truth: The Road to Reconciliation*, The Official Truth and Reconciliation Commission website, <http://www.doj.gov.za/trc/>, accessed 13 November 2007.

there is a significant movement for reconciliation with the indigenous inhabitants of the land, including a formal national process of reconciliation initiated in 1991. Similar work for indigenous reconciliation is taking place in New Zealand and other countries. In these movements, the emphasis is not reduced to the juridical but necessarily seeks a true healing for victims and offenders, with a view to beginning the nation afresh while yet memorialising the true history of the community.

These movements resonate strongly with Catholic practice. The need to name evil and speak truthfully of what has transpired parallels the act of confession in the *Rite of Penance*. Similarly, reconciliation requires contrition and sorrow for the wrongdoing, which is, in turn, authenticated by actions and policies of reparation akin to acts of penance. Finally reconciliation is incomplete unless it is accepted by the victims, itself a form of absolution. This common 'wisdom' should give further impetus to Catholics to be involved in these societal acts of reconciliation.

The Churches themselves have recently begun to offer public apologies for past injustices and inaction in the face of wrongdoing and injustice. On a number of occasions Pope John Paul II offered apologies for the behaviour and inaction of the Catholic Church. Similar apologies have been made by other religious groups as well. These are important reminders to the church and its leadership that the Body of Christ is continually in need of purification and reform, and constitute a sign to society in general that Christians are serious about reconciliation.

Yet these apologies have not been without controversy, from both inside the church and outside. Members of the church have found it difficult when such a divinely inspired organisation admits to complicity in wrongdoing. Others, from within the church community and from society in general, have felt that the apologies either have not gone far enough, have not 'named' the wrongdoings clearly, or have not been followed up by suitable acts of regeneration and reparation. These tensions reflect the difficulties encountered when a person or groups take the path towards reconciliation. They emerge more acutely when we seek to take up a role in resolving atrocities that occurred in history long past or when we are responding to the environmental damage done to the earth by humans as a whole. Nevertheless the tensions and difficulties that emerge are a reminder to the church that it has promoted a powerful and energising dynamic in its ritual framework of contrition, confession, penance and absolution.

From forgiveness to reconciliation

It is worth highlighting a key feature of the Truth and Reconciliation process in South Africa, one also found in the restorative justice approach which brings offenders and victims into contact. This is the importance of victims speaking face to face with offenders about the impact of the crimes they have committed. It is a process that allows the offenders to accept responsibility for their actions and their effects, offering them a chance to embrace wholeness and healing. Further it allows victims to give voice to their deep hurt and private grief, enabling their suffering and pain to be acknowledged by the community in general and providing them the opportunity to regain their dignity and shake off their victimhood.

Such a process has, as well, a further possibility. Once the truth has been told to the offender, and the impact of crime, injustice and violence brought to light, there is a new possibility: that the victim will forgive the offender and they will be reconciled to one another. It takes enormous courage both for the victim to forgive and for the offender to accept this. Yet, here is reconciliation at its fullest, with both victim and offender walking together along the path of healing and wholeness.

Towards a contemporary spirituality of penance

We have, then, the possibility of a new spirituality of penance. Taking its cue from the movements of contrition, confession, penance and absolution, Christians are invited to create a spirituality that is willing to hear the 'voice' of victims, to bring victim and offender together, and to work to bring victims to the point where they are able to forgive. This echoes words attributed to Nelson Mandela: 'Without forgiveness there can be no reconciliation.'

Conclusion

Rites of reconciliation do matter. They bring to the faithful the peace and reconciliation that Christ offers from God. In doing this they lead the baptised into ways of forgiveness and compassion, godly ways, spirit-filled ways, teaching the paths of peace and offering fellow travellers hope and insight into peace-making and reconciliation. Our rites are a gift to all humanity. Their history also opens us to learn from all humanity, inviting us to build divinely inspired rituals from the quest for forgiveness embedded deep in human cultures and societies. The history of forgiveness is not closed but necessarily open to new insights and discoveries. For Christian communities and the human community as a whole rites of reconciliation continue to matter.

Glossary

Absolution

One of the four key elements in the *Rite of Penance*, absolution is a sign of God's pardon and offers the heart the healing experience of complete forgiveness.

Confession

One of the four key elements in the *Rite of Penance*, confession is the act of a heart openly acknowledging sin and fault in the face of God's mercy. Within the *Rite of Penance* it refers to the act of confessing one's sins to a priest. More properly, however, there are three senses of the word 'confession': the confession of faith, the confession of praise, and the confession of sin.

Contrition

One of the four key elements in the *Rite of Penance*, contrition signifies heartfelt sorrow and aversion towards the sin committed.

Penance, satisfaction

One of the four key elements in the *Rite of Penance*, acts of penance are undertaken as a remedy for the effects of sins committed and a help to renewal of life. While the word 'penance' now carries a sense of punishment, the original

Latin word, *paenitentia*, actually meant 'conversion of heart'.

Penitential spirituality

In the face of everyday sin, a way of living based on ongoing conversion and a deepening appreciation of the freedom and grace of one's baptism. This spiritual approach reflects the deepest sense of penance as 'conversion of heart'.

Public penance

A rite of penance developed in the first four centuries of the church. In this ritual form the sinner made a request to undertake a public penance to the bishop, and, at the same time, confessed his or her action to him. It is the penance that was public, not necessarily the preceding sin. The bishop then set an appropriate discipline or penance, often lasting many years and including harsh elements. When the penance was completed the bishop reintegrated the public penitent into the community at a special rite. Often this rite was held on Holy Thursday.

Ransom

Because the payment of a ransom brought freedom, the expression was used in Jesus' time to denote liberation. The payment of a ransom, then, is an important way of describing the experience of forgiveness and reconciliation with God. However it is crucial to recognise that this way of speaking is quite meaningless when pushed to explain the mechanics of how God has freed us. God is God and does not owe or pay a ransom to anyone! It is not a term that can be applied to God's actions but rather it is an expression of how we feel when we realise that sin no longer controls us, that we have been forgiven and reconciled.

Reconciliation

The first Christians had the overwhelming sense that in Christ any perception that God was hostile to them for sin was at an end. Indeed, they felt that the sense of God's friendship had replaced their feeling of enmity, and that a new time of harmony between God and humans had commenced. They realised that this change in them was entirely God's work but one now entrusted to the Christian community: 'In Christ God was reconciling the world to himself, not counting their trespasses against them, and entrusting the message of reconciliation to us' (2 Cor 5:19).

Rite of Penance

The official ritual book that contains the current Catholic rites of reconciliation. It contains four rites: the 'Rite of Reconciliation of Individual Penitents' (the 'first' rite), the 'Rite of Reconciliation of Several Penitents with Individual Confession and Absolution' (the 'second' rite), the 'Rite of Reconciliation of Several Penitents with General Confession and Absolution' (the 'third' rite) and non-sacramental Penitential Services (*Rite of Penance*, Appendix 2 – the 'fourth' rite).

Salvation

Christians believe that all aspects of sin and evil, including their own sin and all aspects that are part of human history and culture and natural events, are taken up and given meaning, peace and reconciliation in Christ.

Satisfaction

See Penance.

Further Reading

The Rite of Penance. Translation by the International Commission on English in the Liturgy (ICEL).

Brown, Neil. 'The Communal Nature of Reconciliation: Moral and Pastoral Reflections'. *The Australasian Catholic Record* 77 n. 1 (2000): 3-9.

Collins, Mary, and David Power, eds. 'The Fate of Confession'. *Concilium* 190 n. 2 (1987).

Crichton, J.D. *The Ministry of Reconciliation: A Commentary on the Order of Penance.* London: Geoffrey Chapman, 1974.

Dallen, James. *The Reconciling Community: The Rite of Penance.* New York: Pueblo Publishing Company, 1986.

Elich, Tom. 'Communal Reconciliation in Pre-Reformation England: Lessons from the Seven-Sacrament Fonts of East Anglia'. *Studia Liturgica* 36 n. 2 (2006) 138-65.

Floristan, Casiano, and Christian Duquoc, eds. 'Forgiveness'. *Concilium* 184 n. 2 (1986).

Gleeson, Gerald. 'The Future of the "Third Rite" of Reconciliation'. *The Australasian Catholic Record* 77 n. 1 (2000): 20-31.

Gusmer, Charles W. *And You Visited Me: Sacramental Ministry to the Sick and the Dying.* Studies in the Reformed Rites of the Catholic Church, VI. New York: Pueblo Publishing Company, 1989.

Jordan, Elizabeth. *Reconciling Women: A Feminist Perspective on the Confession of Sin in Roman Catholic Tradition*. Strathfield: St Pauls, 2000.

Kennedy, Robert J., ed. *Reconciling Embrace: Foundations for the Future of Sacramental Reconciliation*. Chicago: Liturgical Training Publications, 1998.

Moore, Gerard. 'Reconciliation in Our Land and the Liturgical Tradition of Penance'. *Compass* 33 n. 3 (1999): 9-13.

Moore, Gerard. 'The Forgiveness of Sins: A Ritual History.' *The Australasian Catholic Record* 77 (2000): 10-19.

Moore, Gerard, ed. *A Hunger for Reconciliation: In Society and the Church*. Strathfield: St Pauls, 2004.

O'Loughlin, Frank. *The Future of the Sacrament of Penance*. Strathfield: St Pauls, 2007.

Osborne, Kenan B. *Reconciliation and Justification: The Sacrament and its Theology*. New York/Mahwah: Paulist, 1990.

Poschman, Bernhard. *Penance and the Anointing of the Sick*. London, Burns and Oates: 1964.